# Weekly Planner Notebook
## *for*
# *Girls*
## *on the*
# Go

Activinotes

*Activinotes*

DAILY JOURNALS, PLANNERS, NOTEBOOKS AND OTHER BLANK BOOKS

Copyright 2016

Name: ......................................................................................................

Address: ......................................................................................................

E-mail: ......................................................................................................

Contact nos.: ......................................................................................................

......................................................................................................

# • This Week •

| Schedule | | | | | | |
|---|---|---|---|---|---|---|
| **M** | **T** | **W** | **TH** | **F** | **S** | **S** |
| | | | | | | |

| School | Home |
|---|---|

★ _____     ★ _____

★ _____     ★ _____

★ _____     ★ _____

★ _____     ★ _____

| Materials to Prepare | Email/Calls/Follow-Up | Reminders |
|---|---|---|
| ● _____ | ● _____ | ● _____ |
| ● _____ | ● _____ | ● _____ |
| ● _____ | ● _____ | ● _____ |
| ● _____ | ● _____ | ● _____ |
| ● _____ | ● _____ | ● _____ |

| Errands/Home/Personal | Upcoming To Do | Notes |
|---|---|---|
| ● _____ | ● _____ | ● _____ |
| ● _____ | ● _____ | ● _____ |
| ● _____ | ● _____ | ● _____ |
| ● _____ | ● _____ | ● _____ |
| ● _____ | ● _____ | ● _____ |
| ● _____ | ● _____ | ● _____ |

# • Check List •

| Shopping List | Kids List |
|---|---|

★ _____  ★ _____

★ _____  ★ _____

★ _____  ★ _____

★ _____  ★ _____

★ _____  ★ _____

★ _____  ★ _____

★ _____  ★ _____

★ _____  ★ _____

★ _____  ★ _____

| Dinner Dates | Play Dates |
|---|---|

# WEEKLY PLANNER

Monday

Tuesday

Wednesday

Thursday

Friday

Saturday

Sunday

NOTES

# • This Week •

| Schedule | | | | | | |
|---|---|---|---|---|---|---|
| M | T | W | TH | F | S | S |
| | | | | | | |

| School | Home |
|---|---|

★ _____  ★ _____

★ _____  ★ _____

★ _____  ★ _____

★ _____  ★ _____

| Materials to Prepare | Email/Calls/Follow-Up | Reminders |
|---|---|---|
| ● _____ | ● _____ | ● _____ |
| ● _____ | ● _____ | ● _____ |
| ● _____ | ● _____ | ● _____ |
| ● _____ | ● _____ | ● _____ |
| ● _____ | ● _____ | ● _____ |

| Errands/Home/Personal | Upcoming To Do | Notes |
|---|---|---|
| ● _____ | ● _____ | ● _____ |
| ● _____ | ● _____ | ● _____ |
| ● _____ | ● _____ | ● _____ |
| ● _____ | ● _____ | ● _____ |
| ● _____ | ● _____ | ● _____ |
| ● _____ | ● _____ | ● _____ |

# • Check List •

| Shopping List | Kids List |
|---|---|

★ _____
★ _____
★ _____
★ _____
★ _____
★ _____
★ _____
★ _____
★ _____

★ _____
★ _____
★ _____
★ _____
★ _____
★ _____
★ _____
★ _____
★ _____

| Dinner Dates | Play Dates |
|---|---|

# WEEKLY PLANNER

Monday

Tuesday

Wednesday

Thursday

Friday

Saturday

Sunday

NOTES

# WEEKLY PLANNER

Monday

Tuesday

Wednesday

Thursday

Friday

Saturday

Sunday

NOTES

# • This Week •

| | Schedule | | | | | |
|---|---|---|---|---|---|---|
| **M** | **T** | **W** | **TH** | **F** | **S** | **S** |
| | | | | | | |

| School | Home |
|---|---|

★ _____          ★ _____

★ _____          ★ _____

★ _____          ★ _____

★ _____          ★ _____

**Materials to Prepare**          **Email/Calls/Follow-Up**          **Reminders**

● _____    ● _____    ● _____

● _____    ● _____    ● _____

● _____    ● _____    ● _____

● _____    ● _____    ● _____

● _____    ● _____    ● _____

**Errands/Home/Personal**          **Upcoming To Do**          **Notes**

● _____    ● _____    ● _____

● _____    ● _____    ● _____

● _____    ● _____    ● _____

● _____    ● _____    ● _____

● _____    ● _____    ● _____

● _____    ● _____    ● _____

# • Check List •

| Shopping List | Kids List |
|---|---|

★ _____      ★ _____

★ _____      ★ _____

★ _____      ★ _____

★ _____      ★ _____

★ _____      ★ _____

★ _____      ★ _____

★ _____      ★ _____

★ _____      ★ _____

★ _____      ★ _____

| Dinner Dates | Play Dates |
|---|---|

# WEEKLY PLANNER

Monday

Tuesday

Wednesday

Thursday

Friday

Saturday

Sunday

NOTES

# • This Week •

| Schedule | | | | | | |
|---|---|---|---|---|---|---|
| M | T | W | TH | F | S | S |
| | | | | | | |

| School | Home |
|---|---|

★ _____   ★ _____

★ _____   ★ _____

★ _____   ★ _____

★ _____   ★ _____

Materials to Prepare     Email/Calls/Follow-Up     Reminders

● _____   ● _____   ● _____

● _____   ● _____   ● _____

● _____   ● _____   ● _____

● _____   ● _____   ● _____

● _____   ● _____   ● _____

Errands/Home/Personal     Upcoming To Do     Notes

● _____   ● _____   ● _____

● _____   ● _____   ● _____

● _____   ● _____   ● _____

● _____   ● _____   ● _____

● _____   ● _____   ● _____

● _____   ● _____   ● _____

# • Check List •

| Shopping List | Kids List |
|---|---|

★ _____    ★ _____

★ _____    ★ _____

★ _____    ★ _____

★ _____    ★ _____

★ _____    ★ _____

★ _____    ★ _____

★ _____    ★ _____

★ _____    ★ _____

★ _____    ★ _____

| Dinner Dates | Play Dates |
|---|---|

# WEEKLY PLANNER

Monday

Tuesday

Wednesday

Thursday

Friday

Saturday

Sunday

NOTES

# WEEKLY PLANNER

Monday

Tuesday

Wednesday

Thursday

Friday

Saturday

Sunday

NOTES

# • This Week •

| Schedule | | | | | | |
|---|---|---|---|---|---|---|
| **M** | **T** | **W** | **TH** | **F** | **S** | **S** |
| | | | | | | |

| School | Home |
|---|---|

★ _____    ★ _____

★ _____    ★ _____

★ _____    ★ _____

★ _____    ★ _____

| Materials to Prepare | Email/Calls/Follow-Up | Reminders |
|---|---|---|
| • _____ | • _____ | • _____ |
| • _____ | • _____ | • _____ |
| • _____ | • _____ | • _____ |
| • _____ | • _____ | • _____ |
| • _____ | • _____ | • _____ |

| Errands/Home/Personal | Upcoming To Do | Notes |
|---|---|---|
| • _____ | • _____ | • _____ |
| • _____ | • _____ | • _____ |
| • _____ | • _____ | • _____ |
| • _____ | • _____ | • _____ |
| • _____ | • _____ | • _____ |
| • _____ | • _____ | • _____ |

# • Check List •

| Shopping List |
|:---:|

★ _____

★ _____

★ _____

★ _____

★ _____

★ _____

★ _____

★ _____

★ _____

| Kids List |
|:---:|

★ _____

★ _____

★ _____

★ _____

★ _____

★ _____

★ _____

★ _____

★ _____

| Dinner Dates |
|:---:|

| Play Dates |
|:---:|

# WEEKLY PLANNER

Monday

Tuesday

Wednesday

Thursday

Friday

Saturday

Sunday

NOTES

# • This Week •

| Schedule | | | | | | |
|---|---|---|---|---|---|---|
| **M** | **T** | **W** | **TH** | **F** | **S** | **S** |
| | | | | | | |

| School | Home |
|---|---|

★ _____     ★ _____

★ _____     ★ _____

★ _____     ★ _____

★ _____     ★ _____

| Materials to Prepare | Email/Calls/Follow-Up | Reminders |
|---|---|---|
| ● _____ | ● _____ | ● _____ |
| ● _____ | ● _____ | ● _____ |
| ● _____ | ● _____ | ● _____ |
| ● _____ | ● _____ | ● _____ |
| ● _____ | ● _____ | ● _____ |

| Errands/Home/Personal | Upcoming To Do | Notes |
|---|---|---|
| ● _____ | ● _____ | ● _____ |
| ● _____ | ● _____ | ● _____ |
| ● _____ | ● _____ | ● _____ |
| ● _____ | ● _____ | ● _____ |
| ● _____ | ● _____ | ● _____ |
| ● _____ | ● _____ | ● _____ |

# • Check List •

| Shopping List | Kids List |
|---|---|

★ _____  ★ _____

★ _____  ★ _____

★ _____  ★ _____

★ _____  ★ _____

★ _____  ★ _____

★ _____  ★ _____

★ _____  ★ _____

★ _____  ★ _____

★ _____  ★ _____

| Dinner Dates | Play Dates |
|---|---|

# WEEKLY PLANNER

Monday

Tuesday

Wednesday

Thursday

Friday

Saturday

Sunday

NOTES

# • This Week •

## Schedule

| M | T | W | TH | F | S | S |
|---|---|---|----|----|----|----|
|   |   |   |    |   |   |   |

| School | Home |
|--------|------|

★ _____     ★ _____

★ _____     ★ _____

★ _____     ★ _____

★ _____     ★ _____

### Materials to Prepare
- _____
- _____
- _____
- _____
- _____

### Email/Calls/Follow-Up
- _____
- _____
- _____
- _____
- _____

### Reminders
- _____
- _____
- _____
- _____
- _____

### Errands/Home/Personal
- _____
- _____
- _____
- _____
- _____
- _____

### Upcoming To Do
- _____
- _____
- _____
- _____
- _____
- _____

### Notes
- _____
- _____
- _____
- _____
- _____
- _____

# • Check List •

| Shopping List |
|---|

★ _____
★ _____
★ _____
★ _____
★ _____
★ _____
★ _____
★ _____
★ _____

| Kids List |
|---|

★ _____
★ _____
★ _____
★ _____
★ _____
★ _____
★ _____
★ _____
★ _____

| Dinner Dates |
|---|

| Play Dates |
|---|

# WEEKLY PLANNER

Monday

Tuesday

Wednesday

Thursday

Friday

Saturday

Sunday

NOTES

# • This Week •

## Schedule

| M | T | W | TH | F | S | S |
|---|---|---|----|---|---|---|
|   |   |   |    |   |   |   |

| School | Home |
|--------|------|

★ _____    ★ _____

★ _____    ★ _____

★ _____    ★ _____

★ _____    ★ _____

### Materials to Prepare
- _____
- _____
- _____
- _____
- _____

### Email/Calls/Follow-Up
- _____
- _____
- _____
- _____
- _____

### Reminders
- _____
- _____
- _____
- _____
- _____

### Errands/Home/Personal
- _____
- _____
- _____
- _____
- _____
- _____

### Upcoming To Do
- _____
- _____
- _____
- _____
- _____
- _____

### Notes
- _____
- _____
- _____
- _____
- _____
- _____

# • Check List •

| Shopping List |
|---|

★ _____

★ _____

★ _____

★ _____

★ _____

★ _____

★ _____

★ _____

★ _____

| Kids List |
|---|

★ _____

★ _____

★ _____

★ _____

★ _____

★ _____

★ _____

★ _____

★ _____

| Dinner Dates |
|---|

| Play Dates |
|---|

# WEEKLY PLANNER

Monday

Tuesday

Wednesday

Thursday

Friday

Saturday

Sunday

NOTES

# • This Week •

| Schedule | | | | | | |
|---|---|---|---|---|---|---|
| M | T | W | TH | F | S | S |
| | | | | | | |

| School | Home |
|---|---|

★ _____    ★ _____

★ _____    ★ _____

★ _____    ★ _____

★ _____    ★ _____

| Materials to Prepare | Email/Calls/Follow-Up | Reminders |
|---|---|---|
| • _____ | • _____ | • _____ |
| • _____ | • _____ | • _____ |
| • _____ | • _____ | • _____ |
| • _____ | • _____ | • _____ |
| • _____ | • _____ | • _____ |

| Errands/Home/Personal | Upcoming To Do | Notes |
|---|---|---|
| • _____ | • _____ | • _____ |
| • _____ | • _____ | • _____ |
| • _____ | • _____ | • _____ |
| • _____ | • _____ | • _____ |
| • _____ | • _____ | • _____ |
| • _____ | • _____ | • _____ |

# • Check List •

| Shopping List | Kids List |
|---|---|

★ _____  ★ _____

★ _____  ★ _____

★ _____  ★ _____

★ _____  ★ _____

★ _____  ★ _____

★ _____  ★ _____

★ _____  ★ _____

★ _____  ★ _____

★ _____  ★ _____

| Dinner Dates | Play Dates |
|---|---|

# WEEKLY PLANNER

Monday

Tuesday

Wednesday

Thursday

## Friday

## Saturday

## Sunday

## NOTES

# • This Week •

| Schedule | | | | | | |
|---|---|---|---|---|---|---|
| M | T | W | TH | F | S | S |
| | | | | | | |

| School | Home |
|---|---|

★ _____     ★ _____

★ _____     ★ _____

★ _____     ★ _____

★ _____     ★ _____

| Materials to Prepare | Email/Calls/Follow-Up | Reminders |
|---|---|---|
| • _____ | • _____ | • _____ |
| • _____ | • _____ | • _____ |
| • _____ | • _____ | • _____ |
| • _____ | • _____ | • _____ |
| • _____ | • _____ | • _____ |

| Errands/Home/Personal | Upcoming To Do | Notes |
|---|---|---|
| • _____ | • _____ | • _____ |
| • _____ | • _____ | • _____ |
| • _____ | • _____ | • _____ |
| • _____ | • _____ | • _____ |
| • _____ | • _____ | • _____ |
| • _____ | • _____ | • _____ |

# • Check List •

| Shopping List |
| --- |

★ _____
★ _____
★ _____
★ _____
★ _____
★ _____
★ _____
★ _____
★ _____

| Kids List |
| --- |

★ _____
★ _____
★ _____
★ _____
★ _____
★ _____
★ _____
★ _____
★ _____

| Dinner Dates |
| --- |

| Play Dates |
| --- |

# WEEKLY PLANNER

Monday

Tuesday

Wednesday

Thursday

Friday

Saturday

Sunday

NOTES

# • This Week •

| Schedule | | | | | | |
|---|---|---|---|---|---|---|
| M | T | W | TH | F | S | S |
| | | | | | | |

| School | Home |
|---|---|

★ _____    ★ _____

★ _____    ★ _____

★ _____    ★ _____

★ _____    ★ _____

### Materials to Prepare
- _____
- _____
- _____
- _____
- _____

### Email/Calls/Follow-Up
- _____
- _____
- _____
- _____
- _____

### Reminders
- _____
- _____
- _____
- _____
- _____

### Errands/Home/Personal
- _____
- _____
- _____
- _____
- _____
- _____

### Upcoming To Do
- _____
- _____
- _____
- _____
- _____
- _____

### Notes
- _____
- _____
- _____
- _____
- _____
- _____

# • Check List •

| Shopping List | Kids List |
|---|---|

★ _____  ★ _____

★ _____  ★ _____

★ _____  ★ _____

★ _____  ★ _____

★ _____  ★ _____

★ _____  ★ _____

★ _____  ★ _____

★ _____  ★ _____

★ _____  ★ _____

| Dinner Dates | Play Dates |
|---|---|

# WEEKLY PLANNER

Monday

Tuesday

Wednesday

Thursday

## Friday

## Saturday

## Sunday

## NOTES

# • This Week •

| Schedule | | | | | | |
|---|---|---|---|---|---|---|
| **M** | **T** | **W** | **TH** | **F** | **S** | **S** |
| | | | | | | |

| School | Home |
|---|---|

★ _____     ★ _____

★ _____     ★ _____

★ _____     ★ _____

★ _____     ★ _____

| Materials to Prepare | Email/Calls/Follow-Up | Reminders |
|---|---|---|
| ● _____ | ● _____ | ● _____ |
| ● _____ | ● _____ | ● _____ |
| ● _____ | ● _____ | ● _____ |
| ● _____ | ● _____ | ● _____ |
| ● _____ | ● _____ | ● _____ |

| Errands/Home/Personal | Upcoming To Do | Notes |
|---|---|---|
| ● _____ | ● _____ | ● _____ |
| ● _____ | ● _____ | ● _____ |
| ● _____ | ● _____ | ● _____ |
| ● _____ | ● _____ | ● _____ |
| ● _____ | ● _____ | ● _____ |
| ● _____ | ● _____ | ● _____ |

# • Check List •

| Shopping List | Kids List |
|---|---|

★ _____     ★ _____

★ _____     ★ _____

★ _____     ★ _____

★ _____     ★ _____

★ _____     ★ _____

★ _____     ★ _____

★ _____     ★ _____

★ _____     ★ _____

★ _____     ★ _____

| Dinner Dates | Play Dates |
|---|---|

# WEEKLY PLANNER

Monday

Tuesday

Wednesday

Thursday

Friday

Saturday

Sunday

NOTES

# • This Week •

## Schedule

| **M** | **T** | **W** | **TH** | **F** | **S** | **S** |
|-------|-------|-------|--------|-------|-------|-------|
|       |       |       |        |       |       |       |

| School | Home |
|--------|------|

★ _____     ★ _____

★ _____     ★ _____

★ _____     ★ _____

★ _____     ★ _____

### Materials to Prepare

- _____
- _____
- _____
- _____
- _____

### Email/Calls/Follow-Up

- _____
- _____
- _____
- _____
- _____

### Reminders

- _____
- _____
- _____
- _____
- _____

### Errands/Home/Personal

- _____
- _____
- _____
- _____
- _____
- _____

### Upcoming To Do

- _____
- _____
- _____
- _____
- _____
- _____

### Notes

- _____
- _____
- _____
- _____
- _____
- _____

# • Check List •

| Shopping List | Kids List |
|---|---|

★ _____
★ _____
★ _____
★ _____
★ _____
★ _____
★ _____
★ _____
★ _____

★ _____
★ _____
★ _____
★ _____
★ _____
★ _____
★ _____
★ _____
★ _____

| Dinner Dates | Play Dates |
|---|---|

# WEEKLY PLANNER

Monday

Tuesday

Wednesday

Thursday

Friday

Saturday

Sunday

NOTES

# • This Week •

| Schedule | | | | | | |
|---|---|---|---|---|---|---|
| M | T | W | TH | F | S | S |
| | | | | | | |

| School | Home |
|---|---|

★ _____    ★ _____

★ _____    ★ _____

★ _____    ★ _____

★ _____    ★ _____

### Materials to Prepare

- _____
- _____
- _____
- _____
- _____

### Email/Calls/Follow-Up

- _____
- _____
- _____
- _____
- _____

### Reminders

- _____
- _____
- _____
- _____
- _____

### Errands/Home/Personal

- _____
- _____
- _____
- _____
- _____
- _____

### Upcoming To Do

- _____
- _____
- _____
- _____
- _____
- _____

### Notes

- _____
- _____
- _____
- _____
- _____
- _____

# • Check List •

| Shopping List | Kids List |
|---|---|

★ _____
★ _____
★ _____
★ _____
★ _____
★ _____
★ _____
★ _____
★ _____

★ _____
★ _____
★ _____
★ _____
★ _____
★ _____
★ _____
★ _____
★ _____

| Dinner Dates | Play Dates |
|---|---|

# WEEKLY PLANNER

Monday

Tuesday

Wednesday

Thursday

Friday

Saturday

Sunday

NOTES

# • This Week •

| Schedule | | | | | | |
|---|---|---|---|---|---|---|
| **M** | **T** | **W** | **TH** | **F** | **S** | **S** |
| | | | | | | |

| School | Home |
|---|---|

★ _____     ★ _____

★ _____     ★ _____

★ _____     ★ _____

★ _____     ★ _____

| Materials to Prepare | Email/Calls/Follow-Up | Reminders |
|---|---|---|
| ● _____ | ● _____ | ● _____ |
| ● _____ | ● _____ | ● _____ |
| ● _____ | ● _____ | ● _____ |
| ● _____ | ● _____ | ● _____ |
| ● _____ | ● _____ | ● _____ |

| Errands/Home/Personal | Upcoming To Do | Notes |
|---|---|---|
| ● _____ | ● _____ | ● _____ |
| ● _____ | ● _____ | ● _____ |
| ● _____ | ● _____ | ● _____ |
| ● _____ | ● _____ | ● _____ |
| ● _____ | ● _____ | ● _____ |
| ● _____ | ● _____ | ● _____ |

# • Check List •

| Shopping List |
|:---:|

★ _____

★ _____

★ _____

★ _____

★ _____

★ _____

★ _____

★ _____

★ _____

| Kids List |
|:---:|

★ _____

★ _____

★ _____

★ _____

★ _____

★ _____

★ _____

★ _____

★ _____

| Dinner Dates |
|:---:|

| Play Dates |
|:---:|

# WEEKLY PLANNER

Monday

Tuesday

Wednesday

Thursday

Friday

Saturday

Sunday

NOTES

# • This Week •

| Schedule | | | | | | |
|---|---|---|---|---|---|---|
| **M** | **T** | **W** | **TH** | **F** | **S** | **S** |
| | | | | | | |

| School | Home |
|---|---|

★ _____    ★ _____

★ _____    ★ _____

★ _____    ★ _____

★ _____    ★ _____

### Materials to Prepare
- _____
- _____
- _____
- _____
- _____

### Email/Calls/Follow-Up
- _____
- _____
- _____
- _____
- _____

### Reminders
- _____
- _____
- _____
- _____
- _____

### Errands/Home/Personal
- _____
- _____
- _____
- _____
- _____
- _____

### Upcoming To Do
- _____
- _____
- _____
- _____
- _____
- _____

### Notes
- _____
- _____
- _____
- _____
- _____
- _____

# • Check List •

| Shopping List | Kids List |
|---|---|

★ _____
★ _____
★ _____
★ _____
★ _____
★ _____
★ _____
★ _____
★ _____

★ _____
★ _____
★ _____
★ _____
★ _____
★ _____
★ _____
★ _____
★ _____

| Dinner Dates | Play Dates |
|---|---|

# WEEKLY PLANNER

Monday

Tuesday

Wednesday

Thursday

Friday

Saturday

Sunday

NOTES

# • This Week •

## Schedule

| M | T | W | TH | F | S | S |
|---|---|---|----|---|---|---|
|   |   |   |    |   |   |   |

| School | Home |
|--------|------|

★ _____   ★ _____

★ _____   ★ _____

★ _____   ★ _____

★ _____   ★ _____

### Materials to Prepare
- _____
- _____
- _____
- _____
- _____

### Email/Calls/Follow-Up
- _____
- _____
- _____
- _____
- _____

### Reminders
- _____
- _____
- _____
- _____
- _____

### Errands/Home/Personal
- _____
- _____
- _____
- _____
- _____
- _____

### Upcoming To Do
- _____
- _____
- _____
- _____
- _____
- _____

### Notes
- _____
- _____
- _____
- _____
- _____
- _____

# • Check List •

| Shopping List |
|---|

★ _____
★ _____
★ _____
★ _____
★ _____
★ _____
★ _____
★ _____
★ _____

| Kids List |
|---|

★ _____
★ _____
★ _____
★ _____
★ _____
★ _____
★ _____
★ _____
★ _____

| Dinner Dates |
|---|

| Play Dates |
|---|

# WEEKLY PLANNER

Monday

Tuesday

Wednesday

Thursday

## Friday

## Saturday

## Sunday

## NOTES

# • This Week •

| Schedule | | | | | | |
|---|---|---|---|---|---|---|
| M | T | W | TH | F | S | S |
| | | | | | | |

| School | Home |
|---|---|

★ _____    ★ _____

★ _____    ★ _____

★ _____    ★ _____

★ _____    ★ _____

| Materials to Prepare | Email/Calls/Follow-Up | Reminders |
|---|---|---|
| ● _____ | ● _____ | ● _____ |
| ● _____ | ● _____ | ● _____ |
| ● _____ | ● _____ | ● _____ |
| ● _____ | ● _____ | ● _____ |
| ● _____ | ● _____ | ● _____ |

| Errands/Home/Personal | Upcoming To Do | Notes |
|---|---|---|
| ● _____ | ● _____ | ● _____ |
| ● _____ | ● _____ | ● _____ |
| ● _____ | ● _____ | ● _____ |
| ● _____ | ● _____ | ● _____ |
| ● _____ | ● _____ | ● _____ |
| ● _____ | ● _____ | ● _____ |

# • Check List •

| Shopping List | Kids List |
|---|---|

★ _____    ★ _____

★ _____    ★ _____

★ _____    ★ _____

★ _____    ★ _____

★ _____    ★ _____

★ _____    ★ _____

★ _____    ★ _____

★ _____    ★ _____

★ _____    ★ _____

| Dinner Dates | Play Dates |
|---|---|

# WEEKLY PLANNER

Monday

Tuesday

Wednesday

Thursday

**Friday**

**Saturday**

**Sunday**

**NOTES**

# • This Week •

## Schedule

| M | T | W | TH | F | S | S |
|---|---|---|----|---|---|---|
|   |   |   |    |   |   |   |

| School | Home |
|--------|------|

★ _____     ★ _____

★ _____     ★ _____

★ _____     ★ _____

★ _____     ★ _____

### Materials to Prepare
- _____
- _____
- _____
- _____
- _____

### Email/Calls/Follow-Up
- _____
- _____
- _____
- _____
- _____

### Reminders
- _____
- _____
- _____
- _____
- _____

### Errands/Home/Personal
- _____
- _____
- _____
- _____
- _____
- _____

### Upcoming To Do
- _____
- _____
- _____
- _____
- _____
- _____

### Notes
- _____
- _____
- _____
- _____
- _____
- _____

# • Check List •

| Shopping List | Kids List |
|---|---|

★ _____    ★ _____

★ _____    ★ _____

★ _____    ★ _____

★ _____    ★ _____

★ _____    ★ _____

★ _____    ★ _____

★ _____    ★ _____

★ _____    ★ _____

★ _____    ★ _____

| Dinner Dates | Play Dates |
|---|---|
| | |

# WEEKLY PLANNER

Monday

Tuesday

Wednesday

Thursday

Friday

Saturday

Sunday

NOTES

# • This Week •

| Schedule | | | | | | |
|---|---|---|---|---|---|---|
| **M** | **T** | **W** | **TH** | **F** | **S** | **S** |
| | | | | | | |

| School | Home |
|---|---|

★ _____     ★ _____

★ _____     ★ _____

★ _____     ★ _____

★ _____     ★ _____

### Materials to Prepare
- _____
- _____
- _____
- _____
- _____

### Email/Calls/Follow-Up
- _____
- _____
- _____
- _____
- _____

### Reminders
- _____
- _____
- _____
- _____
- _____

### Errands/Home/Personal
- _____
- _____
- _____
- _____
- _____
- _____

### Upcoming To Do
- _____
- _____
- _____
- _____
- _____
- _____

### Notes
- _____
- _____
- _____
- _____
- _____
- _____

# • Check List •

| Shopping List | Kids List |
|---|---|

★ _____  ★ _____

★ _____  ★ _____

★ _____  ★ _____

★ _____  ★ _____

★ _____  ★ _____

★ _____  ★ _____

★ _____  ★ _____

★ _____  ★ _____

★ _____  ★ _____

| Dinner Dates | Play Dates |
|---|---|

# WEEKLY PLANNER

Monday

Tuesday

Wednesday

Thursday

Friday

Saturday

Sunday

NOTES

# • This Week •

## Schedule

| M | T | W | TH | F | S | S |
|---|---|---|---|---|---|---|
|   |   |   |    |   |   |   |

| School | Home |
|--------|------|

★ _____   ★ _____

★ _____   ★ _____

★ _____   ★ _____

★ _____   ★ _____

### Materials to Prepare
- _____
- _____
- _____
- _____
- _____

### Email/Calls/Follow-Up
- _____
- _____
- _____
- _____
- _____

### Reminders
- _____
- _____
- _____
- _____
- _____

### Errands/Home/Personal
- _____
- _____
- _____
- _____
- _____
- _____

### Upcoming To Do
- _____
- _____
- _____
- _____
- _____
- _____

### Notes
- _____
- _____
- _____
- _____
- _____
- _____

# • Check List •

| Shopping List |
| :---: |

★ _____
★ _____
★ _____
★ _____
★ _____
★ _____
★ _____
★ _____
★ _____

| Kids List |
| :---: |

★ _____
★ _____
★ _____
★ _____
★ _____
★ _____
★ _____
★ _____
★ _____

| Dinner Dates |
| :---: |

| Play Dates |
| :---: |

# WEEKLY PLANNER

Monday

Tuesday

Wednesday

Thursday

## Friday

## Saturday

## Sunday

## NOTES

# • This Week •

## Schedule

| M | T | W | TH | F | S | S |
|---|---|---|----|---|---|---|
|   |   |   |    |   |   |   |

| School | Home |
|--------|------|

★ _____     ★ _____

★ _____     ★ _____

★ _____     ★ _____

★ _____     ★ _____

### Materials to Prepare
- _____
- _____
- _____
- _____
- _____

### Email/Calls/Follow-Up
- _____
- _____
- _____
- _____
- _____

### Reminders
- _____
- _____
- _____
- _____
- _____

### Errands/Home/Personal
- _____
- _____
- _____
- _____
- _____
- _____

### Upcoming To Do
- _____
- _____
- _____
- _____
- _____
- _____

### Notes
- _____
- _____
- _____
- _____
- _____
- _____

# • Check List •

| Shopping List | Kids List |
|---|---|

★ _____  ★ _____

★ _____  ★ _____

★ _____  ★ _____

★ _____  ★ _____

★ _____  ★ _____

★ _____  ★ _____

★ _____  ★ _____

★ _____  ★ _____

★ _____  ★ _____

| Dinner Dates | Play Dates |
|---|---|

# WEEKLY PLANNER

Monday

Tuesday

Wednesday

Thursday

Friday

Saturday

Sunday

NOTES

# • This Week •

| Schedule | | | | | | |
|---|---|---|---|---|---|---|
| **M** | **T** | **W** | **TH** | **F** | **S** | **S** |
| | | | | | | |

| School | Home |
|---|---|

★ _____     ★ _____

★ _____     ★ _____

★ _____     ★ _____

★ _____     ★ _____

### Materials to Prepare
- _____
- _____
- _____
- _____
- _____

### Email/Calls/Follow-Up
- _____
- _____
- _____
- _____
- _____

### Reminders
- _____
- _____
- _____
- _____
- _____

### Errands/Home/Personal
- _____
- _____
- _____
- _____
- _____
- _____

### Upcoming To Do
- _____
- _____
- _____
- _____
- _____
- _____

### Notes
- _____
- _____
- _____
- _____
- _____
- _____

# • Check List •

| Shopping List | Kids List |
|---|---|

★ _____   ★ _____

★ _____   ★ _____

★ _____   ★ _____

★ _____   ★ _____

★ _____   ★ _____

★ _____   ★ _____

★ _____   ★ _____

★ _____   ★ _____

★ _____   ★ _____

| Dinner Dates | Play Dates |
|---|---|

# WEEKLY PLANNER

Monday

Tuesday

Wednesday

Thursday

Friday

Saturday

Sunday

NOTES

# • This Week •

| Schedule | | | | | | |
|---|---|---|---|---|---|---|
| M | T | W | TH | F | S | S |
| | | | | | | |

| School | Home |
|---|---|

★ _____
★ _____
★ _____
★ _____

★ _____
★ _____
★ _____
★ _____

### Materials to Prepare
- _____
- _____
- _____
- _____
- _____

### Email/Calls/Follow-Up
- _____
- _____
- _____
- _____
- _____

### Reminders
- _____
- _____
- _____
- _____
- _____

### Errands/Home/Personal
- _____
- _____
- _____
- _____
- _____
- _____

### Upcoming To Do
- _____
- _____
- _____
- _____
- _____
- _____

### Notes
- _____
- _____
- _____
- _____
- _____
- _____

# • Check List •

| Shopping List | Kids List |
|---|---|

★ _____
★ _____
★ _____
★ _____
★ _____
★ _____
★ _____
★ _____
★ _____

★ _____
★ _____
★ _____
★ _____
★ _____
★ _____
★ _____
★ _____
★ _____

| Dinner Dates | Play Dates |
|---|---|

# WEEKLY PLANNER

Monday

Tuesday

Wednesday

Thursday

## Friday

## Saturday

## Sunday

## NOTES

# • This Week •

| Schedule | | | | | | |
|---|---|---|---|---|---|---|
| M | T | W | TH | F | S | S |
|   |   |   |    |   |   |   |

| School | Home |
|---|---|

★ _____      ★ _____

★ _____      ★ _____

★ _____      ★ _____

★ _____      ★ _____

### Materials to Prepare
- _____
- _____
- _____
- _____
- _____

### Email/Calls/Follow-Up
- _____
- _____
- _____
- _____
- _____

### Reminders
- _____
- _____
- _____
- _____
- _____

### Errands/Home/Personal
- _____
- _____
- _____
- _____
- _____
- _____

### Upcoming To Do
- _____
- _____
- _____
- _____
- _____
- _____

### Notes
- _____
- _____
- _____
- _____
- _____
- _____

# • Check List •

| Shopping List |
|:---:|

★ _____

★ _____

★ _____

★ _____

★ _____

★ _____

★ _____

★ _____

★ _____

| Kids List |
|:---:|

★ _____

★ _____

★ _____

★ _____

★ _____

★ _____

★ _____

★ _____

★ _____

| Dinner Dates |
|:---:|

| Play Dates |
|:---:|

# WEEKLY PLANNER

Monday

Tuesday

Wednesday

Thursday

Friday

Saturday

Sunday

NOTES

# • This Week •

| Schedule | | | | | | |
|---|---|---|---|---|---|---|
| **M** | **T** | **W** | **TH** | **F** | **S** | **S** |
| | | | | | | |

| School | Home |
|---|---|

★ _____    ★ _____

★ _____    ★ _____

★ _____    ★ _____

★ _____    ★ _____

| Materials to Prepare | Email/Calls/Follow-Up | Reminders |
|---|---|---|
| • _____ | • _____ | • _____ |
| • _____ | • _____ | • _____ |
| • _____ | • _____ | • _____ |
| • _____ | • _____ | • _____ |
| • _____ | • _____ | • _____ |

| Errands/Home/Personal | Upcoming To Do | Notes |
|---|---|---|
| • _____ | • _____ | • _____ |
| • _____ | • _____ | • _____ |
| • _____ | • _____ | • _____ |
| • _____ | • _____ | • _____ |
| • _____ | • _____ | • _____ |
| • _____ | • _____ | • _____ |

# • Check List •

| Shopping List | Kids List |
|---|---|

★ _____        ★ _____

★ _____        ★ _____

★ _____        ★ _____

★ _____        ★ _____

★ _____        ★ _____

★ _____        ★ _____

★ _____        ★ _____

★ _____        ★ _____

★ _____        ★ _____

| Dinner Dates | Play Dates |
|---|---|

# WEEKLY PLANNER

Monday

Tuesday

Wednesday

Thursday